Love
Dad

This book belongs to

Eloika Harmony

THE ELF
AND
THE DORMOUSE
and Other Faerie Stories

Illustrated by
Bob Petillo

The Unicorn Publishing House
New Jersey

The Elf and the Dormouse

Under a toadstool
   Crept a wee Elf,
Out of the rain
   To shelter himself.

Under the toadstool,
   Sound asleep,
Sat a big Dormouse
   All in a heap.

Trembled the wee Elf,
    Frightened, and yet
Fearing to fly away
    Lest he get wet.

To the next shelter—
    Maybe a mile!
Sudden the wee Elf
    Smiled a wee smile.

Tugged till the toadstool
    Toppled in two,
Holding it over him,
    Gaily he flew.

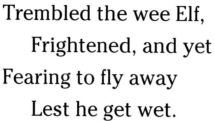

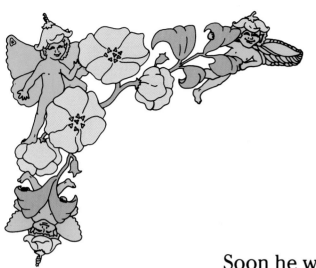

Soon he was safe home,
    Dry as could be.
Soon woke the Dormouse —
    "Good gracious me!

"Where is my toadstool?"
    Loud he lamented.
And that's how umbrellas
    First were invented.

Oliver Herford

The Fairies

The Fairies are a charming folk,
If all the tales be true,
And I believe them ev'ry one,
And doubtless you do, too.
They live in a land enchanted,
With their dear little Queen,
Bewitching in her loveliness,
And dress of silv'ry sheen.

They dance in the fragrant meadows,
    And frolic half the night,
When the moonlight clothes the heavens
    In raiment soft and white.
And carpets all the dells and glens
    With tapestries of gold,
In which are woven diamonds
    Bright in ev'ry length and fold.

And when the mystic clock strikes twelve
    The Cricket's Minstrel Band,
Composed of the Court musicians,
    The greatest in the land,
Send forth its sweetest melody
    From bagpipe, flute, and horn,
In welcome to their Fairy Queen,
    The Daughter of the Morn,

Who comes, with all her maidens fair,
　　To spend the night in mirth,
And dance until another day
　　Is ready for its birth.
But when the light begins to fail
　　In firmament above,
They bid their dainty Queen good-night
　　With words of fondest love.

And then they climb the jeweled arch,
　　Up through the Milky Way,
To kiss the Moon and Stars good-night
　　Ere breaks the dawn of day.
Then scamper down on moonbeams pale
　　Until they reach their home,
Ere God snuffs out the stars' soft light
　　In heaven's matchless dome.

John G. Herndon

The Butterfly's Ball

Come take up your hats, and away let us haste
To the butterfly's ball and the grasshopper's feast;
The trumpeter gadfly has summoned the crew,
And the revels are now only waiting for you.

On the smooth shaven grass, by the side of the wood,
Beneath a broad oak that for ages has stood,
See the children of earth, and the tenants of air,
For an evening's amusement together repair.

And there came the beetle so blind and so black,
Who carried the emmet, his friend, on his back;
And there was the gnat, and the dragon-fly too,
With all their relations, green, orange, and blue.

And there came the moth in his plumage of down,
And the hornet in jacket of yellow and brown,
Who with him the wasp his companion did bring,
But they promised that evening to lay by their sting.

And the sly little dormouse crept out of his hole,
And led to the feast his blind brother the mole,
And the snail, with his horns peeping out from his shell,
Came from a great distance—the length of an ell.

A mushroom their table, and on it was laid
A water-dock leaf, which a table-cloth made;
The viands were various, to each of their taste,
And the bee brought his honey to crown the repast.

There, close on his haunches, so solemn and wise,
The frog from a corner looked up to the skies;
And the squirrel, well pleased such diversions to see,
Sat cracking his nuts overhead in a tree.

Then out came the spider, with fingers so fine,
To show his dexterity on the tight line;
From one branch to another his cobwebs he slung,
Then, quick as an arrow, he darted along.

But just in the middle, oh! shocking to tell!
From his rope in an instant poor Harlequin fell;
Yet he touched not the ground, but with talons outspread,
Hung suspended in air at the end of a thread.

Then the grasshopper came with a jerk and a spring,
Very long was his leg, though but short was his wing;
He took but three leaps, and was soon out of sight,
Then chirped his own praises the rest of the night.

With step so majestic, the snail did advance,
And promised the gazers a minuet to dance;
But they all laughed so loud that he pulled in his head,
And went in his own little chamber to bed.

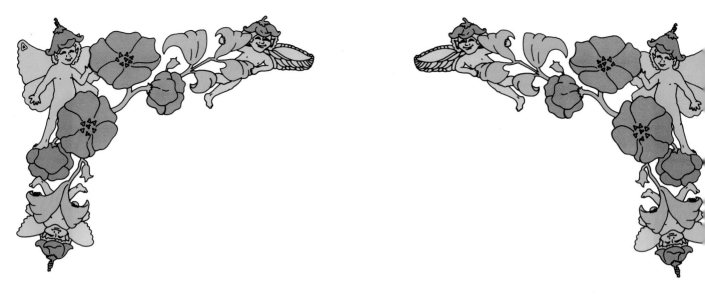

Then as evening gave way to the shadows of night
Their watchman, the glowworm, came out with his light;
Then home let us hasten while yet we can see,
For no watchman is waiting for you and for me.

William Roscoe

The Leprahaun

In a shady nook one moonlit night,
    A leprahaun I spied
In scarlet coat and cap of green,
    A cruiskeen by his side.
'Twas tick, tack, tick, his hammer went,
    Upon a weeny shoe,
And I laughed to think of a purse of gold,
    But the fairy was laughing too.

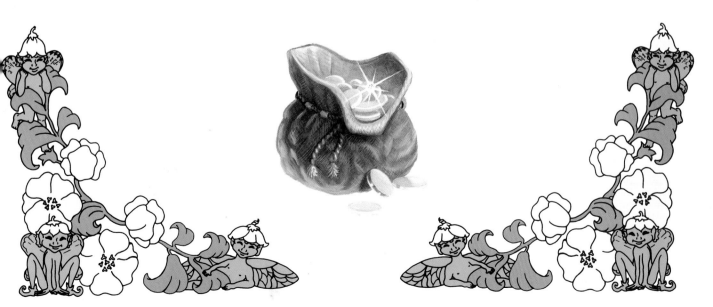

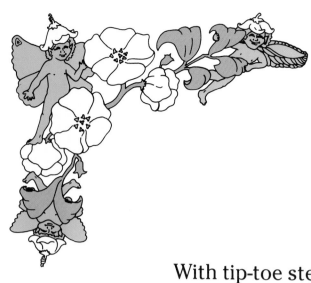

With tip-toe step and beating heart,
    Quite softly I drew nigh.
There was mischief in his merry face,
    A twinkle in his eye;
He hammered and sang with tiny voice,
    And sipped the mountain dew;
Oh! I laughed to think he was caught at last,
    But the fairy was laughing, too.

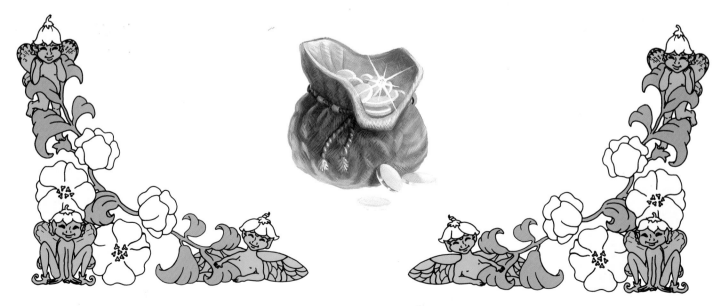

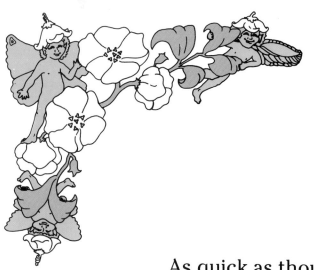

As quick as thought I grasped the elf,
    "Your fairy purse," I cried,
"My purse?" said he, "'tis in her hand,
    That lady by your side."
I turned to look, the elf was off,
    And what was I to do?
Oh! I laughed to think what a fool I'd been,
    And, the fairy was laughing, too.

Roger Dwyer Joyce

Thank you to my family and friends who delved into
the Realm of Faerie while posing for me in this edition of
The Elf and the Dormouse.

CAST OF CHARACTERS

Elf—Laura Petillo
Faerie Queen—Sandy Siggins
The Maiden Faeries—Brie Schagelin
Amanda Branagan
Kristy Siggins
Amy Meisner
Marisa Meisner
Minstrel Band Director—Randy Rice
Other Wee Folk—Bob Petillo
Robbie Suydam
Kevin Suydam
Bob Smith
Leprahaun—Abraham Elias

Editor: John Ingram
Art Director: Heidi K.L. Corso
Printed in U.S.A.
© 1990 The Unicorn Publishing House. All Rights Reserved
Art Work © 1990 Bob Petillo. All Rights Reserved
No copyrighted elements of this book may be reproduced in whole or in part, by any means, without written permission.
For information contact, Jean L. Scrocco,
Unicorn Publishing House, 120 American Road, Morris Plains, NJ 07950

Printing History 15 14 13 12 11 10 9 8 7 6 5 4 3 2 1

Library of Congress Cataloging-in-Publication Data

The Elf and the Dormouse and Other Faerie Stories/illustrated by Bob Petillo.
p. cm. – (Through the Magic Window)
Summary: Presents four illustrated poems: "The Elf and the Dormouse," "The Fairies," "The Butterfly's Ball,"
and "The Leprahaun."
ISBN 0-88101-064-2: $9.95
1. Children's poetry, American. 2. Fairy poetry, American. 3. Children's poetry, English. 4. Fairy poetry, English.
[1. Fairies–Poetry. 2. American poetry–Collections. 3. English poetry.] I. Petillo, Bob, 1949- ill. II. Series.
PS586.3.E44 1990

811.008'09282–dc20

89-39474
CIP
AC

Other Delightful Stories
Richly Illustrated in Our
Through The Magic Window Series:

THE OWL AND THE PUSSYCAT
WYNKEN, BLYNKEN, AND NOD
THE EMPEROR'S NEW CLOTHES
PETER COTTONTAIL'S SURPRISE